Humility

A Spiritual Way of Life

MD Hanley

Copyright

Forward

Humility: A Spiritual Way of Life is a companion book to "Acceptance" and "Gratitude" books in "A Spiritual Way of Life" series. Humility is a conscious act of viewing ourselves with "all the lights on". Looking at ourselves with honesty and courage is difficult. It isn't meant to be an exercise of feeling weak or vulnerable, it is a key to help us to unlock the love for ourselves and our love for others. This brings us a closer connection with God.

Recognizing that we aren't God and are infallible is a huge step in learning how to keep our ego and pride in balance with our "true" selves. This paves the way for a spiritual living and makes us more open and relatable with other people in our lives. Pride and ego can cloud this view of ourselves, but we can also turn pride and ego into confidence and purpose in our lives.

Open yourself up to allow the fact that everyone in the world is unique and different. These differences are the perfect opportunity for us to expand our knowledge and understanding. We can find new insights and perspectives in understanding the differences and also we might help someone else gain a new perspective. Ironically, it's a two-way street in the process of understanding these differences. It's important to remember just as we are on our own spiritual path, everyone else is also on a similar path at a different point than we might be.

Humility is a key component of growth and is a key compliment to Gratitude and Acceptance. The reward is a stronger and more realistic sense of self and a state of congruency of our mind and our actions. I encourage you to embrace humility in your own life. It can help you to grow and develop as an individual, and it can also help you build stronger relationships with others. You will find Humility will produce more happiness, positive emotions, confidence, and well-being.

1.

Why should you strive for humility? If you have been humbled by something, or someone, you might interpret this situation as you being "humiliated" which is often considered a weakness. But on the contrary, real humility is a sign of strength, confidence, and character. Humility makes your relationship with God and other people that much richer and stronger.

CHARACTER
Relationships
Richer and stronger
Why?
God
relationship with God
Strong
Power
Relationship with God
NOT HUMILIATION
Humbling
humbleness
Authentic relationships
True humility
SIGN OF STRENGTH
Confidence
WHY HUMILITY?
Strive for God
Sign of confidence
HUMBLING
humility
TRUE HUMILITY
SIGN OF CONFIDENCE
Strong relationship with God
Real humility
Why humility?
Strive for humility
VALUE OF HUMILITY
Character

2.

Humility is "a modest view of one's own importance, or having the quality of being humble". Humiliation is "the feeling of being ashamed or losing respect for yourself, or an occasion when you have this feeling". The greatest difference between humiliation versus being humble has to do with autonomy. Being humble is an individual's choice while being humiliated is a situation an individual is thrust into by another.

3.

Humility requires unflinching honesty. Absolute honesty with our "true" selves can be one of our hardest challenges, but it can also be the secret needed to unlock our inner strength, peace, awareness and confidence. In a conversation with God, ask God for the strength and the courage to be honest with Him and yourself. God is all knowing and has infinite wisdom.

Honest with him
Peace
Talk with God
Confidence
God has infinite wisdom
Peace
True self
Strength
It is hard to do
God is all knowing
Be honest
Confidence
Secret
Unlock peace
God is infinite
It is hard to do
Be true to yourself
Be honest
Ask God for Courage
Absolute honesty
God is infinite
Unlock peace
Ask God for strength
Honesty
Awareness
Unflinching honesty
Peace
True self
Secret
Secret to humility
Secret
Absolute honesty
Honest with him
Unlock awareness
Talk with God
Unlock you inner strength
Unlock your confidence!
Confidence
God is all knowing
Be honest
Unlock awareness
Peace
Unflinching honesty
Be true to yourself
Ask God for strength
Peace
Unlock you inner strength
Ask God for strength
Talk with God
Confidence
Awareness
It is hard to do
Secret
Honest with him
True self
Honesty
Secret to humility
Strength
Strength
Talk with God
Secret
Absolute honesty
Unflinching honesty
Unlock your confidence!

4.

God is perfect and without flaw. Before we can start on the path of humility, we need to know and accept we aren't perfect and without flaws. We recognize our limitations and admit we need help and support.

Acceptance
We need to accept ourselves
Admit we need help
God is perfect
Recognizing our limitations
Admit we need support
God is without flaw
Truth is acceptance
Path to humility
We ARE NOT perfect
We ARE NOT without flaw
Start on the path
See our truth
As we are
Accept ourselves

5.

Humble individuals are empathetic and considerate of others' feelings, experiences, and needs. They recognize that everyone has something to offer and respect others' opinions promoting more inclusive and supportive relationships. Listen closely to other opinions and ideas, you might find something truly unique which you didn't understand before.

6.

Building empathy helps us cultivate humility. Empathy can help break our pattern of self-focus and connect us to others.

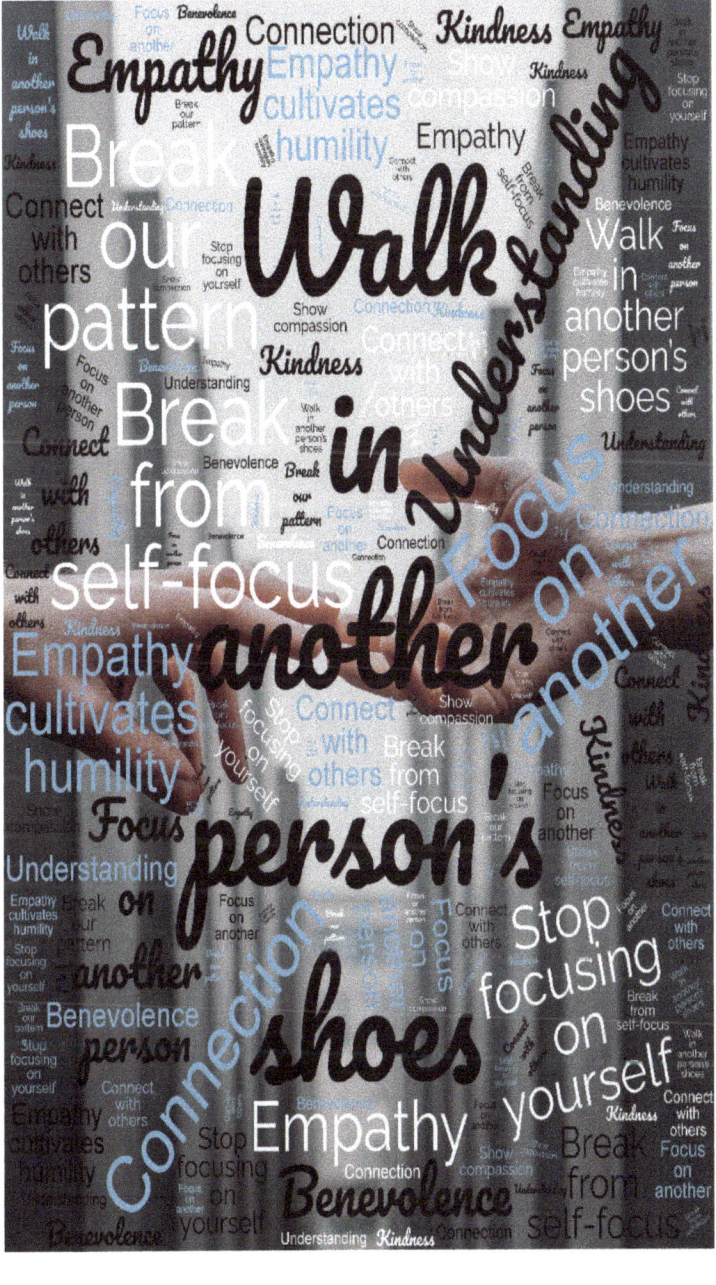

7.

Humble people are grateful for what they have and the people in their lives. They do not take their blessings for granted and recognize that others have contributed to their success.

Respect
Thank you!
Attitude of appreciation
Polite
Blessings
Appreciation
Please
Happy to be alive
Grateful
Happy for the smallest thing
Gratitude
Respect
Others have contributed
Polite
Appreciate what you have
Attitude of appreciation
Success
Appreciate what you have
Gratitude
Happy for kindness
Others have contributed
Success
Gratitude

8.

A humble person does not seek attention or praise for their accomplishments. They recognize that their achievements are the result of hard work, support from others, and sometimes even luck. An honest appraisal of your strengths and weaknesses helps you to be more confident. An honest appraisal also won't allow you to be unassertive or self-deprecating of your true self. When confidence, truth, and awareness are in balance, we are humble.

9.

Humble individuals are always looking to improve themselves. They understand that there's always room for growth if we are willing to put in the work to achieve it. Ask God to help you learn from your mistakes. If we don't learn from our mistakes we will keep repeating them.

10.

Ask yourself, "Am I treating other's as I would want to be treated?" Treating others as you would want to be treated promotes respect, kindness, and compassion, helping to avoid harm, conflict, and injustice.

11.

When we interact with someone who is different from us, we immediately spot their differences. They might be from a different place in the world, or have a different color of their skin, or even a different way of dressing. We become consciously aware of this! When you encounter someone who is different from you, think instead, "What can I learn about this other person?"

12.

Humility is an attitude of spiritual modesty that comes from understanding our place in the larger order of things. It entails not taking our desires, successes, or failings too seriously. We only have one way of seeing the world and there are many other valid and important perspectives from people across races. Humility fosters a lifelong self-examination of racial biases and a willingness to learn from others.

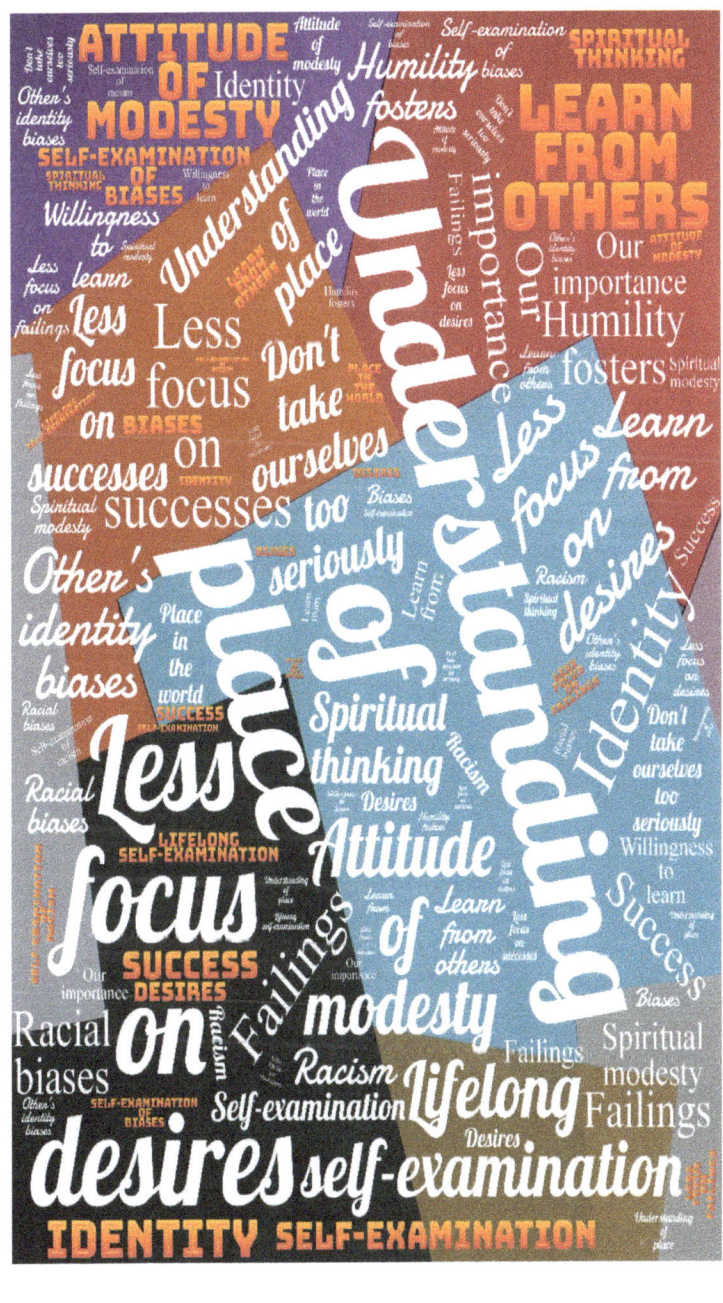

13.

Our DNA does indeed make us unique but it doesn't determine how we choose to develop our strengths and weaknesses. At the root of being human we're all born with the same levels of potentiality. Is a baby with a different skin color inherently "wrong" or different in the way they show love, how they share, care for others, or experience joy? Can a baby from a different part of the world have more anger, hatred, vengeance, or be any different from your child or the child born down the street?

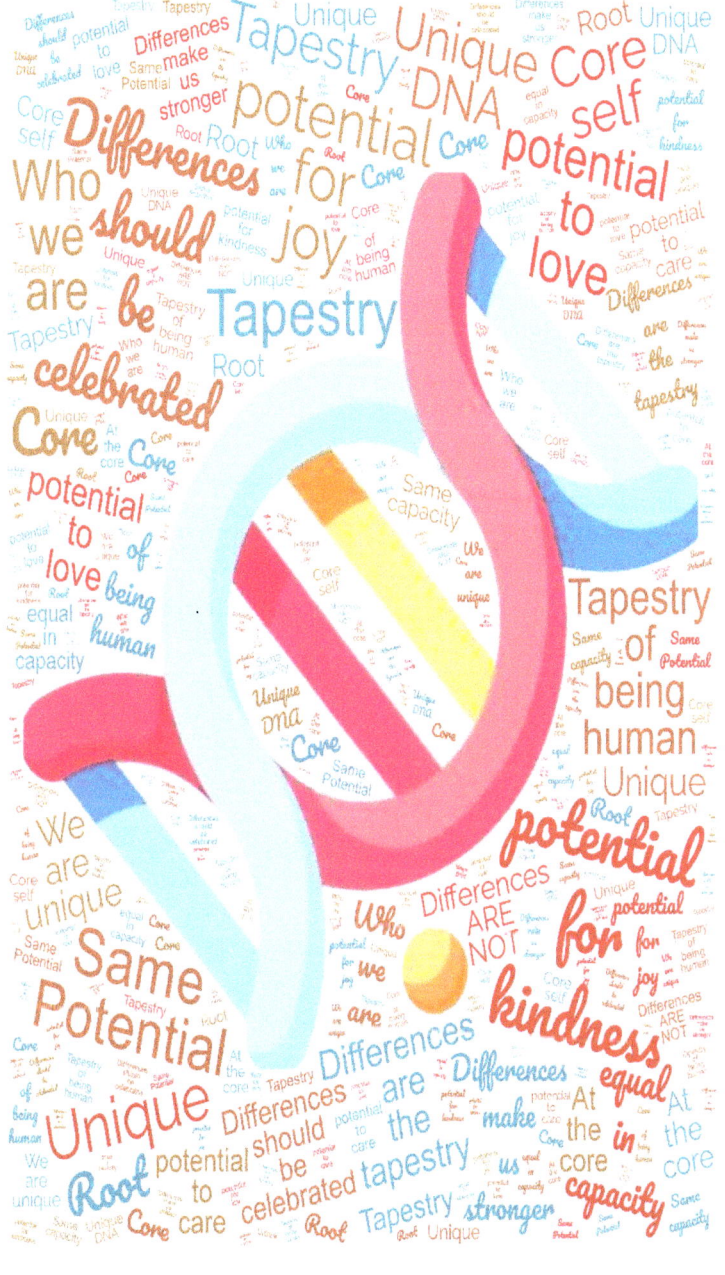

14.

We all have our own biases and assumptions about gender, sexuality, and relationships. Having a sense of humility means acknowledging that we don't know everything and that we may have biases that affect our understanding of gender identity, sexual identity, or cultural identity.

15.

By being aware of our biases, we can work to overcome them and better understand the experiences of others. This means supporting their right to love who they want, expressing their identity without fear, accessing health care and education without barriers, and participating in society without exclusion.

Equality
Right To Express
Access
Predisposition
Aware Of Biases
Awareness
Experience Of Others
Overcome Biases
Better Understand
Right To Not Fear
Experience Of Others
Right To Not Be Excluded
Right To Access Health Care
Self-Aware
Supporting Others
Not Be Excluded
Right To Love Who They Want
Support People
Overcome Biases
Supporting Others
Participate
Right To Express Identity
Preconceived Notion
Right To Love Who They Want
Right To Not Be Excluded
Access
Right To Express Identity
Supporting A Person's Right
Be Aware
Right To Express Identity
Right To Access Health Care
Better Understand
Right To Not Fear
Not Be Excluded
Right To Express
Biases
Self-Aware
Right To Not Fear
Participate
Supporting A Person's Right
Preconceived Notion
Participate
No Exclusion
Not Be In Fear
Biases
Supporting A Person's Right
Overcome Biases
Aware Of Biases
Preconceived Notion
Not Be In Fear
Right To Access Education
Predisposition
Right To Not Be Excluded
Right Participate In Society
Experience Of Others
Not Be In Fear
Right To Access Education
Right To Access Education
Right To Access Health Care
Better Understand
Right Participate In Society
Be Aware
Self-Aware
Supporting A Person's Right
Supporting Others
Right To Love

16.

Having a sense of humility also means respecting the identity of others, even if they differ from us. It means recognizing that everyone's experiences and identities are valid and worthy of respect, and that we should not judge others based on our own assumptions or beliefs. A person's cultural, sexual, or gender identity can also help us support those who may face prejudice and discrimination for their nonconformity.

17.

Practicing humility and understanding the different identities can both help balance and increase our understanding of all people as complex and unique individuals. Acknowledging their dignity, opinions, contributions, and differences means treating them with courtesy, politeness, sensitivity, and assertiveness. It means listening to them and valuing them as human beings.

18.

Humility is not something we do just once. It is a constant pattern of behavior which expands our knowledge of ourselves. We learn by paying attention to how we interact with other people on a daily basis. The benefit we receive from this constant effort is a stronger sense of exactly who we are on the inside and the outside.

19.

What does true humility require? A constant tuning and rebalancing of our minds, our attitudes, and our biases with regard to our actions and our behaviors. If we think too much of ourselves we are arrogant; if we think too little of ourselves we are self-deprecating. Finding this balance is when we have the right amount of confidence in our strengths and weaknesses. When we have scrutinized them, we find the right amount of humility.

20.

Humility is difficult for most human beings and I doubt it can be practiced absolutely by many, if any of us. It requires a secure sincerity and integrated sense of oneself, self-love, compassion and emotional maturity that's often absent, particularly in cases of addiction, and ongoing mental disorders.

21.

Because addiction causes many humiliating and devastating situations for the addict, humility becomes a necessary component for recovery. No one likes to lose control over their life. Admitting to the addiction is the first step to recovery. Because addicts become powerless over their lives and their lives become unmanageable, they humbly ask God for help.

22.

Usually, the way out of addiction involves a "spiritual awakening" when the addicted person asks God for help. Then, they surrender by turning their life and will over to the care of God as they understand Him. They come to believe that a power greater than themselves can return to a normal, sane life.

23.

A humble person accurately acknowledges both their strengths and limitations. They have the capacity to be honest and are without pretense in relation to themselves. They are "right sized" and without false pride, arrogance, or more importantly, damaging low self-esteem. They are modest and without inflated "ego", they are authentic and real, and can admit to their vulnerability.

24.

How do I know what my place is in the universe? Imagine if you had a chance to meet and know each and every person on the Earth. You would find people that you would admire and want to emulate. You would also see people that are still trying, like you, to learn their own place. For each and every person, allow that person to be on the same journey that you're on. Just like you, finding their place amongst the seven billion people on this planet.

25.

When we cultivate humility within ourselves, we can then see more clearly the virtues of others. All the virtues and vices are interrelated and may be said to be "contagious". One virtue encourages other virtues, just as vices often encourage other vices. This is especially true of the virtue, humility, and its opposite, pride, which attracts greed and corruption of the spirit.

26.

Humility is the key to all other virtues. It's the necessary foundation for growth in all the others. If we do not know ourselves—if we cannot see our flaws and strengths (but especially our flaws)—clearly, how can we grow in virtue? How can we begin to make ourselves less and God more?

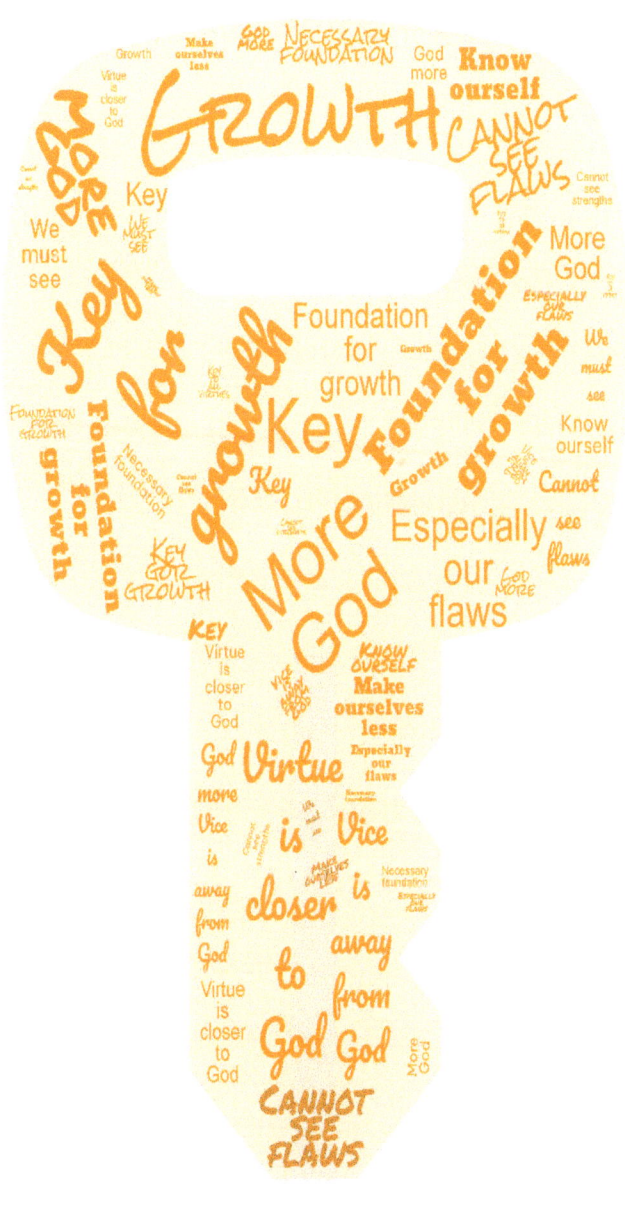

27.

By recognizing that all people are created by God, and that all have inherent worth and dignity, we can develop a sense of humility and empathy towards others. Respecting all people means acknowledging their dignity, opinions, contributions, and differences. It means treating them with courtesy, politeness, sensitivity, and assertiveness. It means listening to them and valuing them as human beings.

28.

A humble person can avoid the pitfalls of pride and arrogance. By recognizing that all good things come from God, and that one's own achievements and accomplishments are ultimately dependent on His grace, individuals can develop a sense of humility and gratitude.

29.

Humility is viewed as a great virtue by most religious traditions. In Christianity, humility is seen as a necessary step for submission to God. A similar view of humility is held in Islam. In fact, the word Islam can be defined as humbly submitting to God. In Buddhism, this attribute is viewed as a key element that people need to develop if they hope to achieve Nirvana. It is sometimes claimed that if a religion is not making the individual humble, they must be doing something wrong.

30.

By recognizing the greatness and majesty of God, individuals can develop a sense of humility and gratitude towards Him. By recognizing that God is the ultimate authority, and that one's own desires and ambitions may not always align with His plan, individuals can develop a sense of humility and acceptance.

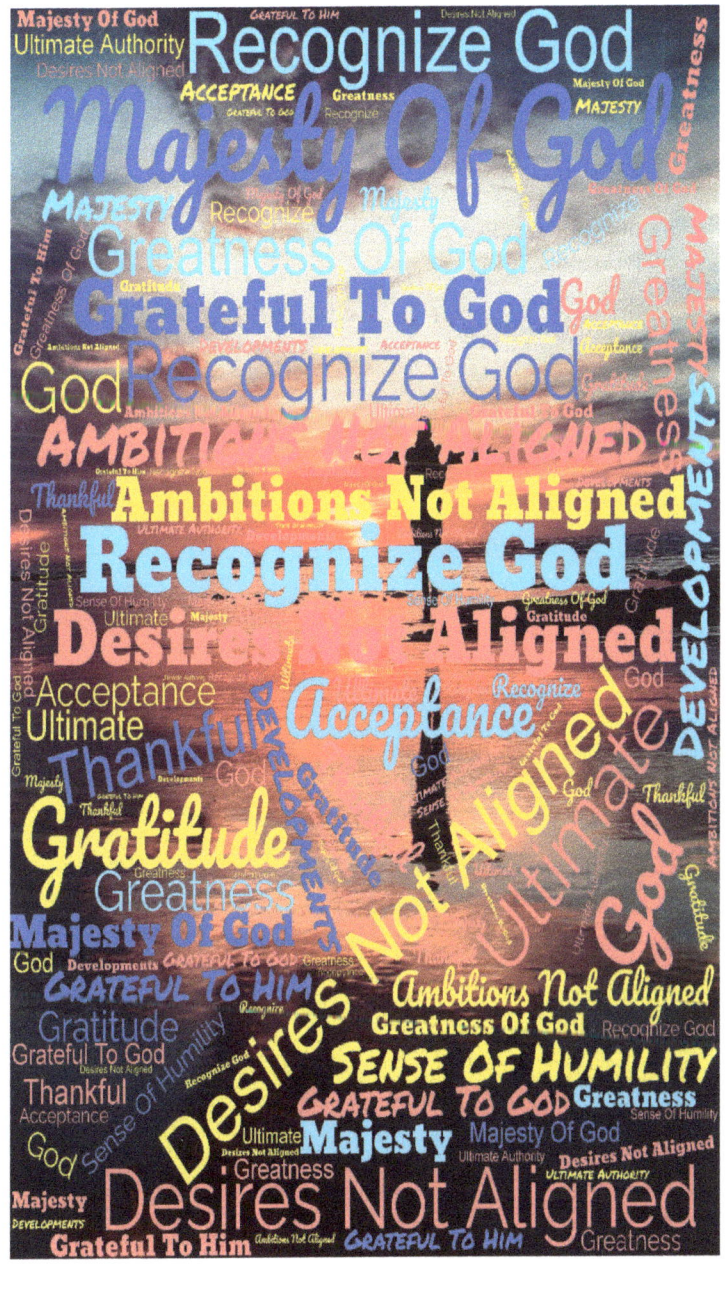

31.

When we exhibit genuine humility in our relations with others, we will almost always find it reciprocated, sometimes in quite marvelous and surprising ways. And there is nothing which disarms a potential foe as effectively as real humility.

32.

True humility is always spontaneous and attractive. True humility always remembers that the gifts and talents we possess are not our own - they are gifts from God. False humility, on the other hand, forgets about God's presence in our gifts. False humility is pridefulness in disguise, it's easy to detect and is always unattractive. True humility gives glory to God while false humility gives glory to self.

33.

In its purest form, humility is simply having a realistic view of yourself and your limitations—knowing that you don't know everything. If you feel that you know every solution to every problem then you're never allowing yourself to be incorrect. Being human is being imperfect and we all carry our own faults and wrong thinking. Saying "I don't know" gives you an opportunity to learn and see a different point of view.

34.

To be truly humble means to recognize our weaknesses and failings honestly. It also means to recognize our strengths, giftedness and blessings with equal honesty. When we use this lens to see ourself, it is only then that we can relate to others authentically, and see in others their own giftedness and blessings.

35.

Humble individuals are never short of friends. They are just so easy to be around that people cherish their company. The fact that they are so modest and respectful means that they rarely come into conflict with anybody. Those who are arrogant tend to rub people the wrong way and cause problems for themselves.

36.

Our ego tries to defend itself from shame, rejection, insecurity (emotional, physical and social), low self-worth, trauma, loss, and emotional wounding. These painful states of being create FEAR.

37.

What do we do to escape this pain? Some of our fear based defenses are anger, anxiety, self-centeredness, controlling behaviors, dishonesty, depression, avoidance and social isolation.

38.

Arrogance makes it difficult for people to learn anything new, because they think they already have all the answers. They fear that admitting to not knowing something will make them look foolish or show ignorance. Arrogance is often combined with ignorance. Until you are able to get beyond these defense mechanisms, you will remain stuck. The perfect way to combat arrogance is to learn humility.

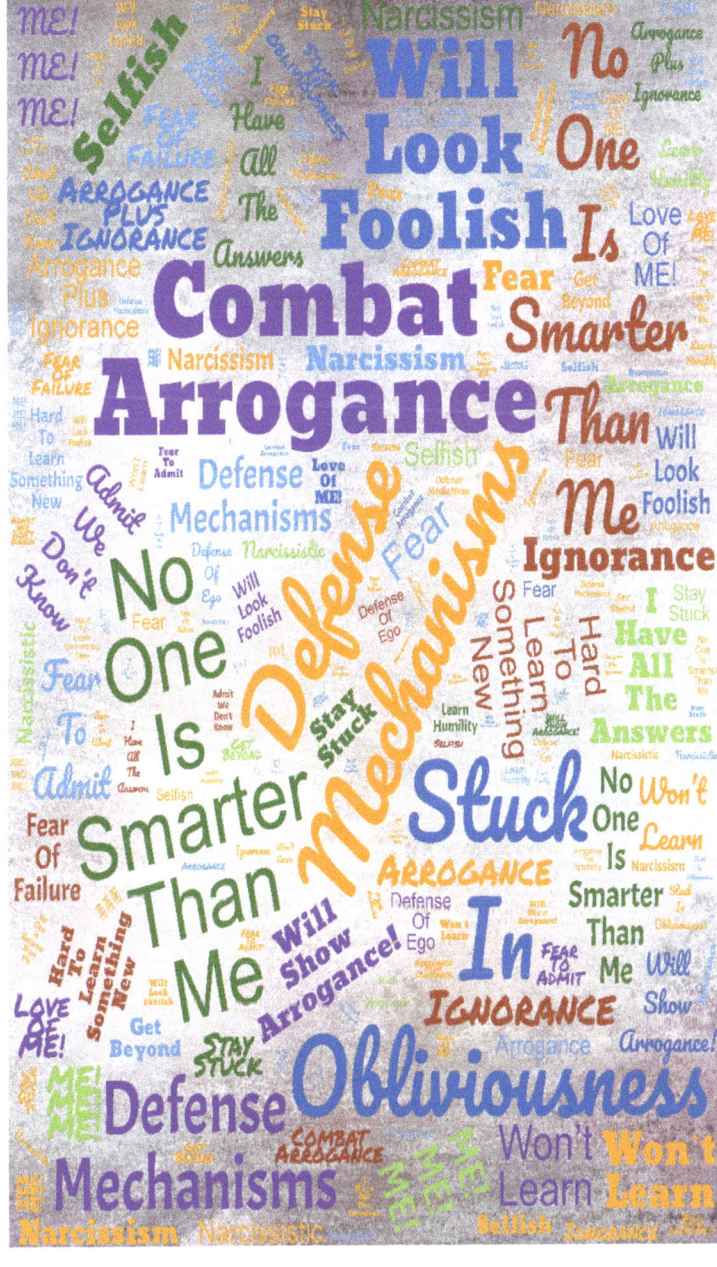

39.

Do you get anxious when you ask questions? People who ask questions may feel foolish for a few moments, but people who never ask questions will always remain ignorant.

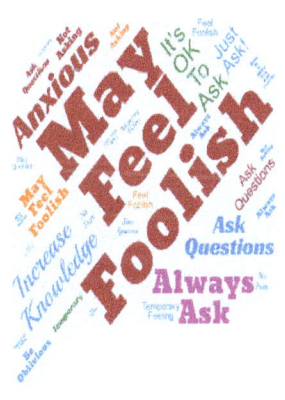

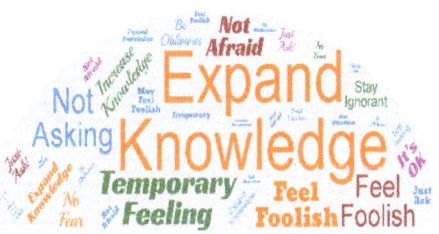

40.

Humility involves being reflective about our own strengths and weaknesses, biases and assumptions, and impact on others. By examining our own behavior and attitudes of how we interact with others, we can identify areas for improvement, address blind spots, and model self-awareness and accountability for the people in our life.

41.

A humble person recognizes that they don't have all the answers and that we can benefit from the expertise and input of others. By approaching decision-making with humility, we can engage with others in a collaborative problem-solving, valuing their insights and ideas, and fostering a sense of ownership and accountability with people.

42.

In Christianity, humility is seen as a central virtue that is closely linked to faith in Jesus Christ. Humility is seen as a key characteristic of Jesus Christ himself. Christians believe that Jesus, despite being the Son of God, chose to humble himself and become human, even to the point of dying on the cross for the sins of humanity.

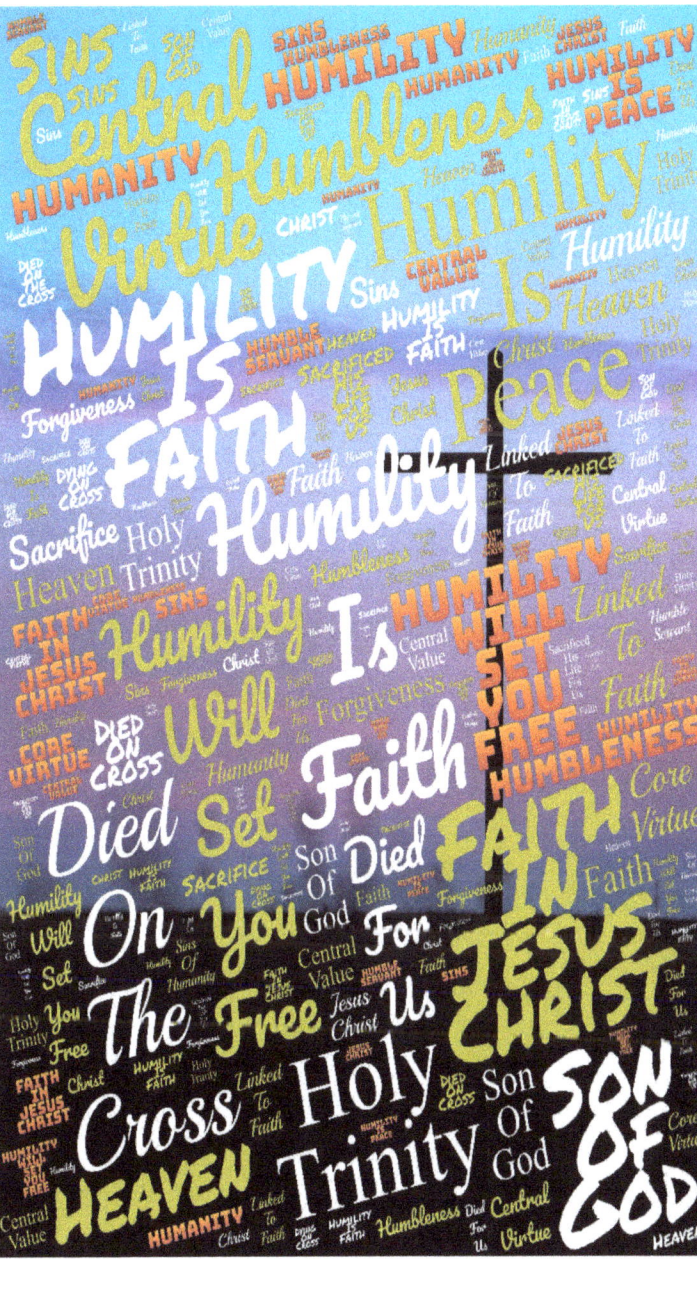

43.

Humility is seen as a way to draw closer to God through faith in Jesus. Christians believe that by recognizing their own limitations and weaknesses, and by trusting in the grace and mercy of Jesus, they can develop a deeper relationship with Him. Christians believe that by recognizing the worth and value of all people, and by serving others with humility and love, they can follow in the example of Jesus.

44.

Humility doesn't have a beginning or an end. It's a constant awareness of who you are at any given moment. Some days you might feel you have a good handle on how you feel with respect to your knowledge of yourself and others. Somedays, you might feel like you are overwhelmed with pride and ego. That's okay! Just reading this and thinking about humility is an action down a path to finding and living a more spiritual way of life. Let's walk down that path together!

ALPHA AND OMEGA
Living
Living A Spiritual Way Of Life
Being
Core
Okay!
It's
No End
No Beginning
Humility
Awareness
Constant
Start The Path
Start Down The Path
Who We Are
Overwhelmed
Feel Overwhelmed
Path To Finding
Walk Down The Path
Pride And Ego
At Any Moment.
Spiritual Way Of Life
Alpha And Omega
Moment
PATHWAY
START

— *Notes* —

Notes

— *Notes* —

Also by MD Hanley

Bit By Bit

Carbon Copy

Quantum Mind

Watch for more at my website!

https://www.mdhanley.com/

or

https://www.hanleyadamspublishing.com

Also Available

If you liked **Humility: A Spiritual Way of Life**, you can also find two additional titles on the **A Spiritual Way of Life Series** currently in your favorite bookstore.

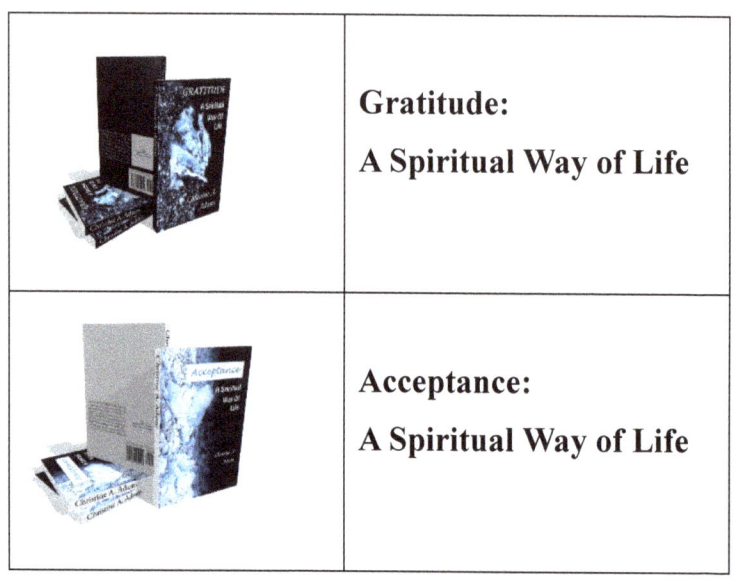

	Gratitude: **A Spiritual Way of Life**
	Acceptance: **A Spiritual Way of Life**

Go to

https://www.hanleyadamspublishing.com

to link to your favorite bookstore.

About the Author

I have been working and consulting in the software engineering field for the past 30 years. I started working in technical support and eventually ended up as a Development Manager and Director of Engineering managing several software development, systems engineering, and QA teams around the world. The exciting part of technology is how it's constantly changing. It never gets dull or boring!

Being an avid reader since I was a little kid, I have always had a passion for storytelling and writing. Having a technical background helped with navigating the seemingly endless road of complexities and challenges of self-publishing.

My first book, **Bit By Bit**, came to me as a random story idea while I was scuba diving on Australia's Great Barrier Reef. It took about a year to plan, outline, and write the story. It was an incredible experience to finally complete it. Over the next year, I wrote another technothriller called **Carbon Copy**. I recently completed **Quantum Mind**, as one of the books in the three book series called Quantum Genesis. This book can be read as a stand-alone book or part of the series when Book 1 and Book 3 are published.

An adventurer at heart, some of my hobbies are scuba diving, flying, and hang gliding. Flying through the congested New York controlled airspace, hang gliding off a mountain top, or scuba diving on the Great Barrier Reef has led to some interesting experiences and sights that very few people have the chance to visit.

Anyone can have a great story,
but you need to be a good storyteller
to make it real and inspire imagination.

- MD Hanley

Dedication

To all the people who walk a path of humility and a spiritual way of life.